hs

GREEK MYTHS
and
LEGENDS

Cover illustration by Magali Bardos

First published in Great Britain in 2007 by Zero To Ten Limited
2A Portman Mansions, Chiltern Street, London W1U 6NR

This edition © 2007 Zero To Ten Limited
© Larousse/S.E.J.E.R 2005

British Library Cataloguing in Publication Data:
A CIP catalogue record for this book is available from the British Library.

ISBN 978 1 84089 9514 8

Printed in Malaysia

GREEK MYTHS
and
LEGENDS

ZERO TO TEN

CONTENTS

JASON AND THE GOLDEN FLEECE

There was once a cruel king of the city of Iolcos called Pelias. He had stolen the throne from his brother Aeson. Aeson had a son, named Jason, and sent him into the mountains to keep safe from the wicked Pelias. There Jason was taught by a magical beast known as a Centaur, which was half human and half horse. The Centaur was called Chiron and no wiser teacher ever lived.

When the boy reached adulthood Chiron taught Jason the history of his family. On hearing the sorry tale Jason declared: "Chiron, I must leave and reclaim the throne that belonged to my father!" In the face of such determination Chiron had no option but to let the boy go.

Jason wrapped a leopard skin around his shoulders and set off. He had not gone far when he met an old woman standing on the bank of a wide, swirling river. "Can you help me across?" she asked. Naturally, being a well-mannered young man, Jason agreed. He lifted the woman onto his shoulders and set off.

The water got deeper and deeper. It went past Jason's shoulders and covered his head, but Jason kept going. Then, disaster! Jason's foot got stuck in the mud. He pulled and pulled but he couldn't free it. Fearing he would drown Jason gave one last heave – the laces on his sandal snapped and he was free. Staggering and out of breath, Jason eventually made it to the other side.

3

When Jason had caught his breath he turned to talk to the old woman – but she was gone! Instead, standing there was a proud, beautiful woman. "I am the goddess Hera," she said. "You have proven your courage. Know now that you are under my protection." Jason thanked the goddess and she disappeared in a flash.

Jason set off once again, still missing his sandal.

Jason's arrival in Iolcos was very strange. No one spoke to him; instead the people stood staring at him, muttering under their breath to each other.

"What's wrong with them?" wondered Jason. "I'm only missing a sandal; that's not so strange is it?"

Jason made his way to the palace, as it was the law at that time that all new arrivals had to present themselves to the king. As soon as he reached the palace gates he was stopped by one of the guards. "You have only one shoe! Is the prophecy true?"

"What prophecy?" asked Jason.

"The one that says a man with one shoe shall overthrow the king!" replied the guard.

"So that was why everyone was acting so strange!" thought Jason.

He followed the guard into the throne room.

Pelias knew the prophecy and when he saw Jason he was worried. "Who are you and what do you want?" he asked.

"I am Jason," the young man replied, "the son of your brother Aeson. I have come to reclaim the throne!"

What Pelias lacked in courage he more than made up for in cunning. "I will gladly hand over the throne," he said, "but on one condition. To prove to me you are fit to be king you must bring me the Golden Fleece."

Like many young men Jason was brave and loved adventure too much. "I'll bring you the fleece!" he declared, boldly.

Pelias smiled to himself. The fleece was guarded night and day by a huge serpent that never slept. Many people had lost their lives trying to take it. Jason would die just as those other young men had.

"I give you one month to complete your task," declared Pelias.

The Voyage of the Argonauts

Jason sought out the great designer Argos and asked him to build him a boat. It was made from wood that the goddess Hera had brought from the sacred forest of Dodone. The timber from this forest was magical – the front of the boat could speak and see into the future. When the ship was finished it was named the Argo.

Now an extraordinary boat needs a special crew, and Jason found just that – fifty brave souls willing to join him on his adventure, a band of warriors he called the Argonauts. Hercules was there, the twins Castor and Pollux, and Calais and Zetes, the winged sons of the North Wind. Orpheus, a musician of such talent he could charm the very beasts themselves was there; as was Peleus, the father of Achilles. They did not know what terrors awaited them.

The first port of call for the Argonauts was a small island on the Black Sea to visit its wise king, Phineus. Imagine their surprise when they saw the ruler, starved and in tears. "It is those cursed Harpies!" he cried. "Every day they come and steal my food, before I can take even a mouthful. I am dying of hunger. I beg you please help me."

Just then the Harpies arrived. They looked like large birds, but they had the heads of evil old women. The Argonauts drove them off with their arrows before Calais and Zetes flew after them and brought them down. Fearing for their lives the Harpies swore never to bother Phineus again.

Phineus was so grateful for the Argonauts' help that he told them a great secret. Their journey would take them to some blue rocks. No sooner would a ship get there than the rocks would close shut, crushing the boat to pieces. Phineus told Jason to release a dove when they arrived at the rocks. If the dove flew through unharmed then the Argonauts must follow immediately. If the rocks closed then they must return home.

When the Argonauts arrived at the rocks they did as Phineus told them and released a dove. The bird lived so the Argo edged its way through the deadly rocks unharmed.

The Golden Fleece

The Argo continued on its way to the land of Colchis, where the fleece was to be found. King Aeetes, who was ruler of Colchis, told Jason he could have the fleece – but only if he could complete the tasks the king had set. They sounded impossible. "Your first task," said Aeetes, "is to plough that field. But you must use my fire-breathing bulls to do it. Then you must sow the field with these." Aeetes held up some shiny, black points about the size of a fist. "Dragon's teeth!"

Watching from the shadows was a young woman, Medea, the daughter of Aeetes. As soon as she saw Jason she fell hopelessly in love with him. Knowing what her father was doing she decided to help Jason.

Medea made a potion and, the night before Jason ploughed the field, she went to his room. "Tomorrow you will die," she said, "unless you use this potion."

"However," she continued, "if you use it you must take me away with you when you have the fleece."

Jason agreed.

"Cover your body with the potion," she said, "it will protect you from the bulls. And when you sow the teeth they will turn into soldiers. To defeat them throw a rock onto the ground – it will turn them against each other."

On the day of the tests Jason covered his body in potion as he had been told. The bulls breathed their terrible fire, and although the grass round about burnt in the heat, Jason was unscathed. He grabbed the fearsome bulls by the horns and immediately they were as quiet and docile as lambs. He could then plough the field without difficulty. King Aeetes was dumbfounded! How could his bulls be defeated with such ease? "Never mind," he thought. "The next task will be the undoing of Jason!"

The moment Jason had cast the dragon's teeth on the field the ground began to shake. Everywhere around him soldiers began to spring from the earth. Jason kept his nerve and calmly threw a rock into the middle of this magical army. Immediately the soldiers went to attack the rock and, in their haste to hit it, cut each other down with their murderous blows.

Aeetes was thrown into a rage by Jason's triumph. "Well!" he screamed. "If you are so clever you can get the fleece yourself – but you'll have to defeat the mighty serpent first!"

Jason was joined by Medea. "Hurry!" she said. "My father means to have you dead one way or another. We have very little time to get the fleece!" She took the Argonaut to the tree where the Golden Fleece hung. Coiled around the trunk was a gigantic serpent that watched the warrior's every move. It hissed loudly at Jason, showing him its cruel, curved fangs. But Medea began to sing. It was no ordinary song – it was a spell. Slowly the snake began to close its eyes until finally it was asleep. Jason snatched the fleece from the tree and ran for the Argo.

An Eventful Return

The Argonauts' return was fraught with dangers – including the deadly sirens. These beautiful creatures were half woman and half bird and their enticing song made sailors wreck their boats to get near them. Orpheus saved the day. His songs drowned out the sirens so the crew of the Argo were not tempted to steer to their doom.

Next the Argo had to slip past two monsters known as Charybdis and Scylla without getting too close to either. One could make holes appear in the sea to swallow passing ships. The other had ferocious animals attached to its body that would devour any sailor that came too near.

And when they reached Crete they encountered Talos, a bronze giant which guarded the island. Talos would hurl rocks at ships to sink them. Although Talos seemed unbeatable it had one weak point – there was a nail in one ankle. If this was removed it would die. Medea came to Jason's rescue again. She put a spell on Talos and pulled the nail from its leg, killing the giant.

After all of their adventures and trials the Argonauts eventually returned home. It had been a long journey but they had finally reached Iolcos.

When Jason arrived at the palace triumphant, Pelias had no choice but to give up his throne as he had promised. Jason became king, Medea reigned by his side and the people of Iolcos rejoiced.

THESEUS AND THE MINOTAUR

It happened that Pasiphaë, the wife of King Minos, went mad and fell in love with a bull. With him she bore a child that was half man and half bull and was named the Minotaur. King Minos was so ashamed of his wife's behaviour he had a huge labyrinth constructed and locked the Minotaur in it. The bull fed on human flesh, and as Minos had defeated Athens in a war, every year seven young men and seven young women were taken from Athens to be fed to the bull.

When Theseus, the son of King Aegeus of Athens, reached adulthood he volunteered to be one of the fourteen souls to be sacrificed to the Minotaur. Theseus had no intention of becoming the Minotaur's lunch, however; instead he planned to kill the beast. His father begged him to reconsider as no one had ever returned from the labyrinth. Apart from the fearsome Minotaur, the passages were so long and confusing that it was almost impossible to find a way out. However, Theseus had made up his mind and no one was going to dissuade him. "Don't worry," he told his old father, "when my boat returns I shall hoist white sails to show that I have been successful. You'll be able to see them from miles away." Aegeus also knew that black sails would mean that Theseus was dead.

After a sea journey the Athenians arrived at the palace of Minos. When they saw the cruel King all except Theseus trembled. A young lady was watching the proceedings – Ariadne, the daughter of King Minos. She was as gentle and caring as her father was cold and cruel. So impressed was she with the heroic Theseus that she went down to the cells where the Athenians were being held to talk to him. "Theseus," she whispered, "I am here to help you if you so wish."

"What do you propose?" replied the young man. "When you enter the labyrinth I will give you the end of a long piece of thread," replied Ariadne. "I will hold the reel. To find your way out, all you need do is follow the thread back to me." Theseus thanked Ariadne. "When I leave," he said, "I shall take you with me and we shall get married."

The following day the terrified victims were led to the mouth of the labyrinth. Theseus was at the head of the Athenians, holding tightly to the thread Ariadne had given him. While his countrymen hung around just inside the entrance, Theseus strode into the dark passageways. After wandering around for an hour or so, Theseus was stopped in his tracks by a horrible bellowing noise. He headed for the sound and when he turned the corner he saw in front of him two evil red eyes. It was the Minotaur!

Our hero and the monster threw themselves at each other and a vicious fight ensued. Eventually Theseus managed to grab hold of one of the Minotaur's sharp horns, and pulled with all his might. With a loud CRACK the horn snapped off. The Minotaur bellowed in rage and pain and charged at Theseus. At the last moment Theseus stepped out of the way and stabbed the Minotaur with the horn. The Minotaur roared once more, staggered slightly and then fell to the ground where it breathed its last.

Ariadne could feel the thread twitching and hear the noises from the labyrinth, but did not know which way the fight was going. All was quiet; then Theseus reappeared! He was safe, as were his fellow Athenians. It was the happiest day of her life! Not waiting for Minos to discover what had happened, the Athenians headed for their ship, along with Ariadne.

On the way home the ship stopped for a while on the island of Naxos. Ariadne slept for a while on the beach; but when she awoke, Theseus and the boat had left without her!

Why on earth did Theseus abandon her, the woman who had saved his life? Some say he no longer wanted to get married. Others say he was ordered to by the gods. Whatever the reason, he was gone and Ariadne was heartbroken.

However, Dionysus, the god of wine, had been watching this. He had been in love with Ariadne for years so he dashed to comfort her. She had lost her man, but had found a god.

Theseus was soon nearing Athens, but he had made a grave mistake – he had forgotten to raise the white sails! What made him forget? Was it the gods punishing him for abandoning Ariadne? Or was it grief from being forced to abandon his love? Whatever the reason he approached his home flying sails that announced his death.

His father, Aegeus, patrolled the cliff tops waiting for his son's boat. When he saw the ship with its black sails, he threw himself from the cliffs in despair. When Theseus discovered that his father was dead, he was devastated. So when Theseus was proclaimed king, his first act as ruler was to name the sea in which his father had perished the Aegean in honour of him.

DAEDALUS AND ICARUS

Daedalus was the brilliant architect who, under the orders of King Minos, built the labyrinth that housed the Minotaur. The Minotaur ate human flesh and many Athenians were sacrificed to the monster until it was killed by Theseus. Thankfully, with the help of Ariadne, the good-hearted daughter of King Minos, Theseus succeeded. The young Athenian then fled Crete and Ariadne went with him.

Minos never knew what had really happened that day in the labyrinth. He was unaware that his own daughter had aided Theseus, and presumed that the Athenian had kidnapped her. He also reasoned that the only way Theseus could have got out of the labyrinth was if Daedalus had betrayed Minos by giving him the plans of the labyrinth. Minos decided to punish his architect by imprisoning both him and his son, Icarus, in the very labyrinth Daedalus had created.

Daedalus knew that without a map of the labyrinth escape would be impossible. However, he was a brilliant inventor who found a solution to every problem. Daedalus thought about the problem for a long time and prayed to the heavens for inspiration. Eventually while staring out at the sky it came to him – they would fly out of their prison.

With the aid of a bow and some good fortune, Daedalus managed to shoot two large birds. Then, with great care he and Icarus took the feathers and started to fasten them together with melted wax. Slowly, slowly they began to fashion them into wings for the two of them.

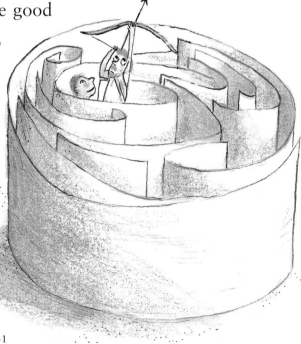

Once the wings were complete, Daedalus fitted them to Icarus and himself. "Now Icarus," he said, "please listen to my advice as it is of the utmost importance. Do not fly too high or too low. If you go too high the sun will melt the wax that holds the wings together. Go too low and the spray from the sea will make the wings too damp. And remember to always keep me in sight."

As soon as the wind was blowing hard enough the two men launched themselves into the air. They were flying! Every so often Daedalus would glance back to make sure that Icarus was alright. Like a young bird leaving the nest for the first time, Icarus was nervous at first but soon gained confidence – too much confidence. Soon he was seeing just how high he could go.

Icarus flew higher and higher. Soon Daedalus had lost sight of him and began to worry. Icarus on the other hand didn't have a care in the world. He was like a god, flying through the air; he felt invincible! "I'll see how close I can get to the sun," he thought, forgetting that he was merely a mortal.

As he flew higher the heat from the sun began to melt the wax that held the feathers in place, just as Daedalus had said it would. The feathers suddenly loosened and the wings fell apart. Frantically Icarus tried flapping his arms, but it is wings that you need to fly, not arms, and the poor boy fell to the ground.

Icarus landed on a small island and was killed instantly. To this day that island is called Icaria in honour of him. Daedalus, who had been powerless to help his poor son, flew down to him. He picked up Icarus' broken body and buried him there.

Daedalus then flew off and sought refuge on the island of Sicily, the home of King Cocalus.

Meanwhile, King Minos – furious at the escape of his prisoners – was scouring the world looking for Daedalus. He too arrived in Sicily and demanded that Cocalus hand Daedalus over if he ever turned up. Daedalus was there already, of course, but Cocalus said nothing. However Minos was suspicious.

Being cunning, Minos had a plan. A while later he returned carrying some thread and a snail shell.

"I shall give a great prize," said Minos, "to the first person who can thread this string through the spirals of this shell."

Many people tried the task, but all failed. Cocalus had seen enough of Daedalus to know that he would be able to figure out how to do it, so he called for the architect to help. Daedalus thought for a while. "I've got it!" he said to Cocalus. "Instruct your servants to bring me some ants."

Daedalus made a small hole in the centre of the shell, and then fastened the thread to one of the ants. He lowered the ant into the hole and waited. Soon enough the ant reappeared out of the mouth of the shell, dragging the thread behind it.

Cocalus was overjoyed and ran to claim his reward. Big mistake! When Minos saw the shell he knew Daedalus was there, for only he was clever enough to solve the problem.

"So did you do this?" asked Minos. "Or was it Daedalus?" Cocalus realised that Minos knew his secret and confessed. He also agreed to bring Daedalus to Minos. Cocalus invited Minos to stay at the palace while he made the arrangements.

Now Cocalus liked Daedalus and knew that Minos was not a good man. So that night, while Minos took his bath, he instructed his daughters to fill it with scalding hot water. Minos died that night in his bath, burnt bright red like a lobster.

Daedalus was so grateful to Cocalus for saving him that he designed and built many fine buildings in his honour.

HERCULES,
THE **GREATEST HERO**

Zeus, the king of the gods, would occasionally fall in love with a human. One time he even disguised himself as the husband of a woman called Alcmene in order to seduce her. When Alcmene saw Zeus she thought her husband had returned from the war and was overjoyed to see him. That night after Zeus had gone her husband Amphitryon really did return home. Nine months later Alcmene gave birth to twins: one child, whose father was Amphitryon, she named Iphicles; the other, whose father was Zeus, she named Hercules.

Now Zeus, being the god of gods, wanted his son to be immortal just like him. For a half-human child to become immortal it had to drink the milk of a goddess. So one night while his wife Hera slept, Zeus took Hercules and tried to get him to drink Hera's milk. Unfortunately for Zeus, Hera woke up and stormed off. Hercules would not be an immortal after all. And unfortunately for him the poor innocent child had made a powerful enemy in Hera.

Hera had realised that Hercules must be Zeus's child and she was half-mad with jealousy and righteous rage. She decided there and then that the child should be wiped from the face of the earth. She summoned up two large snakes and despatched them to kill Hercules. That night the snakes slid into Hercules and Iphicles' cribs and were about to strike with their poisonous fangs when Iphicles woke up. The child screamed in terror which woke his half-brother Hercules. Without a thought Hercules grabbed a snake in each hand and throttled them.

When the twins were seven years old a tutor was called upon to teach them reading, writing, mathematics, and music as well as physical exercises. As good a pupil as Iphicles was, Hercules was equally as bad being inattentive, grumpy and rude.

One day the tutor was utterly fed up and went to strike Hercules. Quick as a flash Hercules hit the teacher first with his stool and killed him outright. The boy was dragged before the courts but it was clear that Hercules had acted in self-defence and was set free.

Hercules' father, Amphitryon, was really quite worried about his unruly son and his super-human strength. He made Hercules leave the palace and learn how to live off the land instead.

Despite this unpromising start, Hercules would grow up to be the greatest of Greek heroes.

THE TWELVE TASKS

When Hercules was still a young man he married Megara and had three children with her. The goddess Hera still disliked Hercules and couldn't abide to see him happy. So one night she put him under a spell that drove him mad – Hercules killed each and every one of his children. When he came to his senses and saw his bloody sword he was distraught. He tried to kill himself but Zeus stopped him. Instead Hercules went to consult the wisest sage of all the ancient Greeks, the Oracle of Delphi, to see how he could atone for his crime. The Oracle said that Hercules had to spend the next twelve years serving King Eurystheus and doing any tasks he set.

Hercules did not know it, but the king had decided that if Hercules was to prove his character and courage he would have to complete twelve tasks, each one more difficult than the last.

1 The Nemean Lion

Eurystheus summoned Hercules and set him his first task. "You must kill the lion of Nemea," said the king, "and bring me back its skin as proof that you have completed your task. But take heed, there is not a weapon made that can pierce its hide."

Hercules made his way to Nemea and soon tracked down the fearsome beast. As soon as Hercules saw it he threw his spear, but it bounced off the lion as if it were made of stone. So Hercules took his club and struck the lion on its head with all his strength.

The beast staggered but did not die and promptly set off for its lair. Hercules threw down his club and ran after it. He caught the lion and wrapped his arms around its neck and squeezed and squeezed until the lion breathed no more.

But now the lion was dead how would Hercules skin it, after all no weapon could cut it? Hercules had an ingenious idea. He used one of the lion's own razor-sharp claws to remove the skin. The job done, Hercules returned victorious to the king wearing the skin of the Nemean Lion.

2 The Hydra of Lerna

The next task Eurystheus set Hercules involved a truly terrifying creature. In the marshes of Lerna there lived a nine-headed monster called the Hydra. Its breath was poisonous and it liked nothing more than to feast on any unwary travellers that might be passing by.

Hercules went to fight the Hydra with his nephew Iolaos. To their horror they discovered that every time they chopped off a head a new one grew back. It was only when Iolaos burnt each new cut to stop the heads growing back that the Hydra eventually died.

Hercules used the Hydra's poison to coat his arrows, just in case they might be useful later.

3 & 4 The Erymanthean boar and the Cerynian hind

The third task the king set Hercules was to capture the huge Erymanthean boar. "Do not take this task lightly," warned the king, "for this is a most aggressive animal." Hercules was not to be beaten and he caught the beast by pushing it into a deep pile of snow which allowed him to bind it. When he brought the boar to the palace the king was so alarmed at the sight he hid in a large pot. Eurystheus ordered Hercules never to bring his living trophies into the palace again, but to leave them outside the doors instead.

The next task was to bring back one of the hinds of the goddess Artemis. The deer the king wanted was the fastest animal alive and Hercules chased the creature for over a year. Eventually the creature was so exhausted by the chase, that Hercules could catch it and bring it back to Eurystheus to complete his task.

5 The birds of Lake Stymphalus

The king decided to send the troublesome Hercules to his certain death with his next task – to rid Lake Stymphalus of its deadly birds. These birds had feathers of steel that they fired like arrows, and beaks and claws of brass which they used to rip people apart. Hercules had no idea what to do until the goddess Athena came to his help. She scared the birds with a pair of cymbals and as they flew into the air Hercules shot them down with his poisoned arrows.

6 The Augean Stables

Hercules' reputation grew with each task he completed and King Eurystheus began to feel foolish. So for his next task he decided to humiliate Hercules to bring him back down to size.

Eurystheus demanded that Hercules clean the stables that belonged to King Augeas in a single day.

The stables were huge and filled with manure. The stench was so bad that whenever anyone got close they quickly beat a retreat in the opposite direction.

King Augeas laughed out loud when Hercules arrived and explained his task. "You are going to clean these stables in a day?" the king asked. "You couldn't do it in a hundred years, never mind a day!" But Hercules had a plan. He went to a nearby river and built a dam out of stones to divert its flow. The river, prevented from travelling its usual course, gushed down the hill and through the stables washing all the manure onto the fields. In no time the stables were so clean you could have eaten off the floor. The king was astounded to say the least.

7 & 8 The Cretan Bull and the Mares of Diomedes

The Cretan Bull was the father of the Minotaur and it was widely feared. Hercules wrestled it until it he had tamed it. When he took the bull to Eurystheus the king was so scared that he released the bull immediately.

Hercules' eighth task was to steal the man-eating horses of King Diomedes. Now Diomedes would feed unwanted guests to his horses, so Hercules wasted no time and captured them that very night.

Diomedes was furious and took his army to capture Hercules. But Hercules was cunning and released the horses that were, by now, starving. They attacked the king and his army and Diomedes was eaten by his own beasts. As soon as the horses were full they became tame and Hercules led them back to Eurystheus.

9 The belt of the queen of the Amazons

It was Eurystheus' daughter who set the next task. She wanted the golden belt of the queen of the Amazons. The Amazons were warrior women, but the son of Zeus charmed them, especially their queen, Hippolyta. But Hera intervened and managed to persuade the Amazons that Hercules intended to steal their queen away from them. Alarmed, they attacked Hercules who fought back and, although he did not want to, he killed many of them, including Hippolyta. He took the belt and completed his task, but was tortured by the memory of it forever.

10 Geryon's Oxen

Hercules' next task was to steal the oxen that belonged to the giant Geryon. He was no ordinary giant, for Geryon had three bodies. What's more, the oxen were also guarded by Geryon's frightening hound. Hercules despatched these two monsters just as he had defeated all the others. But to get home Hercules had to climb the mountain of Gibraltar. Rather than try to get the oxen over the mountain, Hercules split the rock in two, leaving two great pillars which we know today as the Straits of Gibraltar.

11 The Golden Apples from the Garden of the Hesperides

Eurystheus was particularly cunning with Hercules' next task. The king wanted the golden apples that grew in the garden that was tended by the nymphs known as the Hesperides. Now the tree on which these apples grew was a wedding present belonging to the goddess Hera who, as we know, detested Hercules. Our hero knew that the only person who could help him was Atlas, the giant who held up the heavens, because Atlas was also the father of the Hesperides.

When Hercules asked Atlas for help the giant replied: "My daughters will gladly pick the apples, but you had better get me to ask them for you. You hold up the heavens for me while I look for them." So Hercules swapped places with Atlas, but the giant took a long time to come back with the apples. The truth was Atlas quite liked not having to hold up the heavens and had no intention of swapping back with Hercules. "I'll take the heavens back when I've rested a little," lied Atlas. "No problem," replied Hercules, guessing what the giant was up to. "But I'm in an awkward position here, could you hold the heavens for a moment while I get adjusted?" As soon as Atlas had hold of the weight Hercules slipped off, taking the apples with him. Another task was successfully completed.

12 Cerberus, the guardian of Hades

The final task took Hercules down to Hades, the home of the dead. Eurystheus wanted Hercules to bring back Cerberus, the three-headed dog that guarded the entrance to the underworld. Hercules was guided to the river Styx, which formed the boundary of Hades, by the god Hermes. At first Charon, the ferryman who took people across the river, refused to take Hercules because he wasn't dead. Eventually Charon was persuaded and Hercules was allowed over. Our hero went straight to the King and Queen of Hades, where he asked for permission to take Cerberus. They were much amused by the bravery of Hercules. "If you can overpower Cerberus without using weapons," they said, "you can take him." This would be difficult, as Cerberus not only had three heads filled with razor sharp teeth, but a deadly dart at the end of his tail, too.

Hercules was protected by the lion's skin he wore and soon overpowered the beast. He wrapped Cerberus in the skin and carried it back to the world of the living. When King Eurystheus saw the beast he again hid inside a large jar. "Do not fear," laughed Hercules, "if you like I'll take it back to Hades."

The king agreed and
with this final task
complete Hercules was
a free man again.

THE TRAP OF CENTAUR NESSUS

As the days drifted into years Hercules married Deianira and lived life as simply as any other mortal. One day Hercules and his wife came to a fast-moving river. As they pondered how to get across the centaur Nessus appeared. He said to them: "I'll take Deianira on my back, and Hercules you can swim."

They did not realise that Nessus was up to no good. No sooner was he in the water than he tried to steal Deianira away. When Hercules spotted this treachery he shot Nessus with his poisoned arrows. Before Nessus died he whispered to Deianira, "Take some drops of my blood in this vial – if you fear Hercules is falling in love with another woman it will bring him back to you."

Deianaria hid the vial and forgot about it for many years until she saw her husband talking to a beautiful woman. That night she poured the drops of blood onto Hercules' tunic.

Alas, she had fallen right into the centaur's trap. This was not a love potion as she had imagined. Instead it was a powerful poison which fastened the tunic to our hero's skin where it burned into his flesh. Hercules was in such agony that he committed suicide on a funeral pyre.

Now that the mortal part of Hercules was dead, Zeus could welcome his son to Olympus, the home of the gods, where Hercules, too, was now an immortal.

MIDAS OF THE GOLDEN TOUCH

King Midas was as stupid as he was greedy. Despite this he was a king in the land of Phrygia. One day a man was brought to him – he was roaring drunk and had been found wandering around the mountains by some peasants who worked the land. Stupid though Midas was, he instantly recognized the man as Silenas, the tutor and friend of Dionysus the god of wine. It seemed that Silenas had wandered away from a procession to take a nap and when he awoke he didn't know where he was. He had been wandering the countryside for days before he had been discovered by the peasants. Midas showed him due hospitality and took him in and even held a banquet in his honour.

At this point Dionysus arrived looking for Silenas. He was most impressed with the way Midas had treated his companion. "Midas," Dionysus said, "I cannot thank you enough for what you have done and the care you have shown. Please, name your own reward and I will give it to you."

Midas, who placed wealth above everything else, thought for a long time about what would bring him the most riches. Suddenly an idea came to him and he was so excited by his cleverness he asked for it there and then. "I would like everything I touch to turn into gold!" said Midas excitedly. "Are you sure that is wise?" asked Dionysus. "You said I could ask for what I wanted!" retorted Midas, crossly. "And that is what I want!"

So the god granted Midas' wish and when Midas touched the chair next to him it was instantly transformed from wood into shining gold.

Mad with joy, Midas ran about his palace
touching everything he could see: doors; furniture;
columns – everything glittered a brilliant gold and
Midas was overcome with how rich he had become.

Midas spent many happy hours in this fashion until his rumbling stomach told him that it really was time he ate something. He reached out for a bunch of grapes, but they were instantly turned into hard balls of gold. Midas nearly broke his teeth when he tried to eat some bread and when he went to take a drink he found his wine had turned to liquid gold!

Scared by this unforeseen consequence Midas called for his son to show him what was happening. Unfortunately, in his hurry Midas grabbed his son by the arm and the boy was turned into a golden statue there and then. Midas was beside himself with shock and self-pity. How could he live like this? He was hungry and would surely starve to death surrounded by all the wealth his gift and curse had created. He cried out to Dionysus for help, but for a whole day Dionysus ignored him.

Finally the god deigned to appear. "What do you want now, foolish man?" asked Dionysus. "Pity," replied the king. "I beg you to take back your reward, it is nothing but a curse." Dionysus smiled. "Then take yourself to the Pactolus River and immerse yourself in its waters – then everything will be as normal. I hope that this has been a lesson to you, oh greedy Midas." The king did as he was told and sure enough when he emerged from the river all the gold had gone and his son was alive.

And to this day small nuggets of gold can sometimes be found on the bed of the Pactolus river.

The Donkey Ears of Midas

Although Midas no longer loved gold, he was still as stupid as before and this was demonstrated with another mishap. The gods Pan and Apollo were arguing over which of them was the better musician, even though Apollo was the god of music. They decided to have a competition and King Midas went to watch the tournament. Apollo played first and his mastery of the lyre was met with widespread acclaim. When Pan played his pipes the haunting notes were truly beautiful but they were no match for Apollo's playing. The judges gave the verdict to Apollo.

There was only one person in the crowd who was stupid enough to loudly dispute the decision, and guess who it was – King Midas! He went up to the judges and said that his ears had been charmed more by Pan's pipes than by Apollo's lyre. Apollo was offended by the king's outburst. "You stupid mortal!" said the god, "You have the musical taste of a donkey! In fact, you deserve the ears of a donkey!"

Midas heard a great burst of laughter from the crowd. He reached up and felt his head – sure enough he now sported a fine pair of donkey's ears. He ran back to his palace as fast as his legs could carry him and hid the ears beneath the largest hat he could find.

However, after some weeks, Midas was in desperate need of a haircut. He summoned his barber, and threatened him with death if he should tell anyone of the secret of his ears.

For a long time the barber kept his word, but the secret grew inside him until he had to let it out. Not wishing to break his promise, he ran to the river bank and dug a hole in the ground, and told the secret to the hole and buried it. But when reeds grew there they brought the secret up with them and whispered it in the wind so all could hear the tale of the unfortunate Midas.

PYGMALION
AND HIS DREAM WIFE

On the island of Cyprus there lived a man called Pygmalion. He was a great sculptor, but he had refused to marry as he had never found a woman to his liking. "Not beautiful enough," he would think, or, "too tall," or, "too small." With every woman he met he found some flaw. So picky was Pygmalion that he preferred to spend his time in his studio, rather than enjoy himself with other people. Instead he would dream of creating a statue of his ideal woman.

One day he decided to make his dream become a reality. He selected a piece of milk-white ivory and delicately began to chisel away at the block. Slowly, slowly a form began to appear, a woman more beautiful than anything nature itself had ever produced.

Pygmalion, the master-sculptor, stepped back to admire his work. He had done it! He had created his ideal woman. And it had to be said, his carving had been so precise that the statue almost seemed real.

Fascinated, Pygmalion reached out to touch the statue to see if it was really just ivory. Of course it was; but although Pygmalion knew this he found it difficult to believe that the statue wasn't a real person. He kissed it, and gave it a hug, and was sad when it did not respond. He bought it flowers and jewellery and even laid it down on the softest pillows he could find. Pygmalion knew that his behaviour was strange, but he couldn't help himself; he was in love with his own statue.

Some time later, the people on the island of Cyprus held a festival in honour of Aphrodite, the goddess of love. Sacrifices were made and offerings were brought to her temple. When Pygmalion brought his offering and laid it on the altar he prayed to the goddess. "Oh Aphrodite," he said, "I beg you to find me a woman as beautiful as my ivory statue."

Pygmalion returned to his lonely studio. He went to the statue and whispered to it, "I have prayed that Aphrodite find me a woman as beautiful as you." He kissed the statue on the cheek and stood back, alarmed. The skin had felt warm. He reached out with a trembling hand and touched the statue's hand. He wasn't going mad, the skin was warm! He gently kissed the statue on the lips and its eyes opened and its cheeks blushed slightly. Pygmalion was overjoyed and threw his arms around the statue and the statue did the same to him. She was no longer a piece of chiselled ivory, but a real woman!

Pygmalion named her Galatea and they were married with the blessing of Aphrodite, whose magic had transformed Pygmalion's statue. The couple had a daughter, too, and they called her Paphos after the birthplace of the goddess who had made Pygmalion's dream come true.

EROS AND PSYCHE

Psyche was the youngest daughter of a Greek king. She was famous across the land for her great beauty. Young men would travel from far and wide just to catch a glimpse of her. Soon her reputation exceeded even that of Aphrodite, the goddess of love. Now, if there was one thing that the gods didn't like it was being usurped by mere mortals. Aphrodite was furious. She summoned her son Eros for help. "Punish that upstart," Aphrodite commanded, "by making her fall in love with the ugliest person you can find."

Back home in Greece, Psyche was feeling miserable anyway. There wasn't a man around who dared ask for her hand in marriage. Many came to admire her beauty, but all left without a word. The king was beginning to get worried, so he decided to visit the wisest person of all – the Oracle. However the Oracle had terrible news for the king – he would have to deliver his daughter to a monstrous serpent that lived on a nearby hill.

This was not the sort of marriage the king had in mind. In tears he took his daughter Psyche to that hill and in tears he left her there to die.

The Surprise of Love

No sooner had the king left than Zephyrus, the god of the wind, appeared and carried Psyche away. He flew on until he reached a valley and there gently placed Psyche on the ground. In front of her rose a beautiful palace built of crystal and with floors made from precious stones. When Psyche entered she heard a voice. "Welcome," it said, "relax and allow the maidservants to attend to your every whim."

Psyche felt at ease in the palace. She knew that she would come to no harm there. A soothing concert of voices accompanied her as she ate that night.

That evening a man came to her in the darkness.
"Do not be afraid," he said to her in a soft voice,
"I am your husband and I will take care of you. But
do not ask to see my face or you will lose me forever."

The next morning he was gone.

These nocturnal visits continued every night. Psyche loved her new husband and she had no idea it was really Eros, the god of love. He had been smitten by Psyche's beauty and had decided not to carry out his mother's orders.

Psyche and Eros lived like this for many a day and both were happy. One day Psyche said that she would like her sisters to visit as she missed their company. Eros agreed, but begged her not to listen to what her envious sisters might say, and to remember that she must never try to see his face or all would be lost. Psyche promised to remember his words.

Fatal Curiosity

Zephyrus brought Psyche's sisters to the valley. Psyche was overjoyed to see her sisters again and happily showed them round the beautiful palace. There was no joy in the sisters' hearts though, only jealousy. "So what does this husband of yours look like then?" they asked. Psyche saw no need to lie to her own sisters so she admitted that she didn't actually know. This merely fuelled the sisters' spite. "What!" they shrieked. "Then he is obviously a monster. He's probably trying to fatten you up before eating you. Take this knife and when he sleeps tonight light the lamp to see what you're doing and kill him."

Psyche refused to believe her sisters or do as they suggested. However, a small germ of an idea had taken root in her mind. That night, as Eros slept, Psyche took a lamp in her trembling hand and held it near her husband, determined to see what he really looked like. What she saw was the most beautiful creature she had ever laid eyes on. She stared at Eros, entranced; but failed to see a small drop of oil fall from the lamp and land on his shoulder.

Immediately Eros awoke and grabbed his shoulder. "Psyche!" he said. "Why couldn't you listen? Now I must leave and we shall never meet again."

Psyche clung onto Eros but with a shrug he was gone. Psyche collapsed to the ground in despair. The only thing she could think of was to drown herself in the river; but when she went to throw herself in, the waters drained away and a voice said: "Do not give up! Go and find your husband!"

The Persecution of Psyche

Eros, who had been burned by the lamp oil, had returned to his mother, Aphrodite. She was furious with her son and the mortal. She offered seven kisses to the person who could bring Psyche to her. No man could turn down an offer like that and it was not long until the goddess had her prisoner.

When Psyche was brought to Aphrodite, the goddess laughed. "You ugly little girl," she sneered, "Did you think you could be my daughter-in-law? You have burned my son and now you must pay. Sort out this seed before dawn. If you fail, you die."

Psyche looked at the huge pile of mixed seeds and burst into tears. It would have taken years to sort, never mind hours. However, a passing ant took pity on Psyche and with the aid of the other ants in its colony sorted the seeds in record time.

The following morning Aphrodite was astonished to see that the task had been completed. "Well," she said, "that was obviously too easy. In which case, you can fetch me a handful of wool from the golden sheep that live over there."

The sheep with the golden wool were famous for their deadly bite and would allow no one to get near them. Once again Psyche, filled with despair, tried to drown herself in the river. Again a voice spoke to her. "Wait until the sun goes down," it said. "The sheep will come to the river to drink and will have left clumps of wool on the bushes in their field." And so, by following the voice's instructions, Psyche was able to complete her second task.

Enraged by Psyche's success, Aphrodite ordered the young woman down to Hades, the kingdom of the dead, to fetch back a pot of magical beauty cream from Persephone, the queen of Hades. Psyche knew that this was like a death sentence as no one who ventured into Hades ever returned.

Filled with despair, Psyche took herself to the top of a tall tower and made to throw herself off. For the third time she heard a voice. "Psyche," it said, "why do you try to kill yourself? Trust yourself and you shall succeed. See the coins and cakes to your side? Take them for they are gifts for Charon who ferries the dead to Hades across the River Styx; and for Cerberus the fearsome three-headed dog which guards it. If a drowning man calls to you for help do not hold out your hand to him – it is one of Aphrodite's traps. And under no circumstances look into the pot Persephone gives you.

As the voice had said, the coins were all that Charon needed to ferry Psyche across the River Styx and the two flat cakes kept Cerberus at bay. Psyche collected the pot of cream from Queen Persephone and made her way home. She was feeling so tired she sat down for a rest. "My skin feels very dry," she thought, rubbing her face. "Perhaps if I put on just a little bit of this cream I'll look better for my love when I return." No sooner had she opened the pot than a plume of grey smoke escaped and Psyche fell into a deep sleep. It was another of Aphrodite's tricks!

Saved by Love

Eros had scarcely recovered from his injury when he went looking for Psyche and found her lying as if she were dead. He took her in his arms, carefully wiped away the evil spell and carried Psyche to Mount Olympus, the home of the gods. Eros went straight to Zeus, the king of the gods, to ask a great favour – for Psyche to be immortal like him. Zeus knew that Eros was a useful friend, so he granted his request.

All of the gods were invited to a double celebration – Psyche joining the ranks of the immortals and her wedding to Eros. Even Aphrodite came and buried her differences with her son and new daughter-in-law.

Now that there were no secrets or impediments between them they were truly happy and a while later Psyche had a daughter whom they named Volupta.

PHAETON
AND THE **CHARIOT** OF THE **SUN**

Young Phaeton had never known who his father was, until one day his mother revealed it was Helios, the Sun god. Phaeton nearly exploded with pride when he heard the news! From then on he bragged about who his father was. Finally his friends could bear it no longer. "You idiot! Do you believe everything your mother tells you?" they snapped. "But Helios is my father!" Phaeton retorted. "Prove it then," the other children mocked.

His pride pricked, Phaeton stormed to the palace of Helios, but as soon as he came face to face with the Sun god sitting on his sparkling throne, Phaeton's anger was replaced by fear. "Come closer my boy," said Helios. "What do you want?" Phaeton edged forward nervously. "If it is true that you really are my father, then I have come to ask you a favour," he said. Helios smiled upon his son and hugged him tightly. "For my son, anything," he said. "As I am a god, I can grant you anything to prove that I am your father." Phaeton was overjoyed. "Then let me drive your chariot! Just for one day – that'll show everyone I'm your son!"

Helios immediately regretted his promise. Nothing was more difficult, or more dangerous, than driving his chariot. It was pulled by four horses that spat fire from their mouths and fiery nostrils and it travelled each day across the sky to bring heat and light to the Earth. "What you are asking is impossible," said Helios. "You have neither the experience nor the strength to drive my chariot of fire. You're only a child! And a mortal at that. There isn't even another god that knows how to control the horses that pull it. Even Zeus, the king of all gods, wouldn't dare try. Ask for anything else but this!" But proud Phaeton would not listen and in the end Helios was forced to give in.

His heart filled with misgivings, Helios led his son to the chariot, all the while advising Phaeton on how to drive it. "Remember to hold tightly to the reins," Helios said, "or the horses will get away from you. Don't go too high and don't go too low. Remember to always travel to the west, and keep a look out for my track marks, they'll show you the way to go. I beg you one last time, abandon this foolish venture."

Phaeton, filled with the brashness of youth, heard not a word of what his father was telling him. He grabbed the reins and with a crack he was gone. Immediately impetuous young Phaeton realised he didn't know what he was doing. He didn't know how to hold the reins properly or what each horse was called. The flying horses noticed that their driver was not pulling them back as usual. He was lighter too, so the horses soared higher and higher into the sky.

The chariot went as high as the stars and the monsters that lived there. When Phaeton saw the Scorpion with its terrible claws and deadly tail he dropped the reins in fright. The horses, free of any control from the driver, pulled the chariot this way and that across the sky. Sometimes they flew high and sometimes they flew so low that the flames from the chariot burned cities to the ground, incinerated forests and dried up rivers. Wherever the chariot went there was chaos.

Zeus saw what was happening from the top of Mount Olympus and was furious. "That young fool will destroy the Earth the way he is carrying on," he thundered. And he struck Phaeton down dead.

The boy's body landed in a river. There the river nymphs, the Naiads, took the body and buried it. They carved on his tombstone, "Here lies Phaeton, driver of the chariot of the Sun. Though he lacked the ability to do it, he had the audacity to try it."

The horses found their way home by evening, but the next morning Helios was still so upset over the loss of his son that he would not take the chariot out. That day the world remained in total darkness.

ARACHNE'S CHALLENGE

Beware those mortals who compare themselves to the gods! Here is the cautionary tale of Arachne, a young woman who dared to defy the goddess Athena. Arachne lived a modest life in the kingdom of Lydia, but she was the most talented weaver for miles around. The beautiful creations she made on her loom drew admirers from towns and villages from the whole of Greece. People asked her if she was a pupil of Athena, the goddess of weaving.

This hurt Arachne's pride. "Of course not!" she would reply. "I am the pupil of no one. Even Athena wouldn't dare to measure herself against me."

Now Athena heard this and immediately went to Lydia disguised as an old woman. "My dear Arachne," said Athena, "it really will not do to compare yourself to the gods. If you repent now I am sure you will be forgiven." The insolent Arachne paid no heed to the old woman. "Old lady," she replied, "keep your advice for your daughters and grandchildren; I can look after myself. If Athena is so gifted, let her challenge me."

As soon as Arachne said this, Athena flew into a rage. "The time has come!" she said and changed from an old woman into her true form. The looms were prepared and the two weavers went to work. Athena made a tapestry from the finest gold and crimson threads. It showed her victory over Poseidon for the city of Athens. Surrounding it were images of the other gods and in each corner Athena deliberately wove in images of what happens to mortals who compare themselves to the gods: some were turned into mountains, others into birds. The work was magnificent. Athena carefully removed it from her loom and went to display it in front of Arachne.

However, when Athena saw what Arachne had done she was lost for words. She had made a tapestry showing Zeus, the king of the gods, and all the mortal women he had fallen in love with. In one picture it showed Zeus when he turned himself into a bull to carry off Europa. In another scene he was a swan trying to seduce Leda. Such insolence, mocking the affairs of the gods! But what made Athena especially annoyed was that the quality of Arachne's work was well above her own. Although it was only a tapestry on a rough, wooden loom it was so life-like it was almost real.

Athena's Anger

Athena would not be humiliated by a mere mortal any further. In her fury Athena tore up Arachne's tapestry and smashed her loom, before slapping Arachne across her face. Arachne fled, upset at both the blow and at upsetting one of the gods. She went straight to her room and, driven mad with grief, took a thin rope and hung herself. When Athena discovered this sorry sight even she was moved with pity. "You were a brilliant weaver, Arachne," she said. "Seeing you suspended there has given me an idea how you may yet spin for all eternity."

Athena took some plants and made a special potion. She applied it to the body of the dead girl and an amazing transformation took place. Her arms and legs turned black and her body turned into a black ball. From the body came four further legs and from her belly came an endless silken rope. Arachne had been reborn as the first spider – the mother of all spiders who weave and spin to this very day.

PERSEUS
AND MEDUSA

The extraordinary story of Perseus starts well before his birth. Indeed, the tale begins with his grandfather, King Acrisius. An oracle had told him that he would have a grandson, but that this boy would be responsible for the king's death. Acrisius was horrified. What could he do to stop his only daughter, Danae, producing a son? He took a radical step; he locked his daughter in a bronze prison cell with a maid for companionship.

However, Zeus, the king of the gods, saw Danae and fell in love with her. Cunning Zeus then devised a way of entering the prison to see her. One night Danae felt a fine rain of gold fall upon her through the bars in the cell wall. It was Zeus, who had transformed himself into the precious metal to get to her.

Nine months later Danae gave birth to a boy she named Perseus. Now, it is very difficult to bring up a boy without anyone knowing, especially in a prison. One day King Acrisius was walking past the cell when he heard the baby crying within. He entered and demanded to know what was going on. The maid told him that Danae had a son. "Who is the father?" asked Acrisius angrily. When the maid said it was Zeus the king suspected that the maid was teasing him and flew into a rage, killing the unfortunate woman there and then. Fearing that the prophecy would come true, Acrisius locked his daughter and her son in a wooden chest and had it flung into the sea.

The chest did not sink as Acrisius had intended. Instead, it floated off and washed up on the island of Seriphos. Danae and Perseus were rescued there by a fisherman. They stayed for a number of years and Perseus grew into a strong and intelligent young man. A while later, the ruler of the island, a cruel tyrant called Polydectes took a fancy to Danae. She refused his advances, counting on her son to protect her. "She will soon change her mind," thought Polydectes, "if I get rid of her son." So he invited Perseus to a banquet and announced that he would leave Danae alone in exchange for a certain gift – the head of the gorgon, Medusa. Without pausing for thought, the rash young man agreed to the challenge.

But what was a gorgon? Well there were three of these monsters, sisters in fact, each endowed with golden wings, the tusks of boars and instead of hair they had writhing snakes. Worse still, if you looked at them you would be turned to stone! Two of the gorgons were immortal, but one, Medusa, was not.

The next day Perseus realised how rash he had been, so he went to the king and offered him a horse as a gift instead. "No!" cried Polydectes. "You promised me the head of Medusa, and that is what I want." Proud young Perseus did not want to lose face, so he had no choice.

The Head of Medusa

Several men had already set off to kill Medusa, but not one of them had ever returned. Perseus felt desperate. But let's not forget that he was the son of Zeus; and the gods looked favourably upon him, in particular Athena and the cunning Hermes. They told him they would help him to complete his task.

The first thing they told Perseus to do was to find the nymphs, but the only people who knew their whereabouts were the Graeae. They were sisters to the gorgons, but these three had looked old and wrinkled from the day they were born. What's more they had only one eye and one tooth between them. They had to share them whenever they wanted to see something or eat. Consequently they were always squabbling about whose turn it was.

Perseus hid from the Graeae, for even with one tooth, they would have devoured him. He waited until they were passing the eye and tooth amongst themselves and then flew like an arrow and snatched them away. The Graeae demanded them back, but Perseus replied that he would return them only if they showed him the way to the nymphs. They were obliged to accept.

Perseus soon found the home of the nymphs; three creatures as beautiful as the Graeae were terrifying. They told him where he could find Medusa and offered him three objects that would help him in his task: a pair of winged sandals like those of Hermes, which allowed their wearer to fly; a helmet from Hades, the king of the underworld, which could make its wearer invisible, and a bag for carrying the head of Medusa. Hermes looked down on Perseus and gave him a final gift; a sword with a sickle blade capable of cutting through anything.

Now fully equipped, Perseus flew to the island of the gorgons. There was no mistaking the cave where they lived. It was a terrible place, where all around stood the statues of men turned to stone by the sight of the monsters.

Perseus shivered at the sight, but the goddess Athena appeared before him to help. They waited until the two immortal gorgons were asleep and then Athena flew above Medusa, holding her highly polished shield. By looking at the reflection of Medusa in the shield Perseus could see the gorgon without having to look directly at her. The reflection chilled Perseus to the bone, but he steeled himself and advanced on the monster. With one thrust he sliced off Medusa's head. The blood spurted out and from it came a magnificent winged horse, Pegasus. Keeping his eyes on the shield, Perseus picked up the head and put it inside the bag the nymphs had given him. As he fled that terrible place Medusa's sisters awoke and gave chase. Even though they could fly as fast as Perseus, because of the helmet that made him invisible the gorgons couldn't find him.

The Beautiful Andromeda

Perseus flew home on Pegasus, and on the way he noticed a young woman fastened to a rock at the edge of the sea. Captivated by her beauty, Perseus flew down to ask who she was and why she was imprisoned. "It is a long story," she said, her voice broken by sobs. "My name is Andromeda. My mother, Cassiopeia, made a foolish boast – she said that she was more beautiful than the Nereids, the ocean nymphs. Poseidon, the king of the sea, punished us for her folly. He sent a sea monster to ravage our country. An oracle told my father, King Cepheus, that the only way to free us of this curse is for me to be sacrificed.

At that precise moment the monster rose from the waves. As it made its way to Andromeda, Perseus flew over to the beach where Andromeda's parents stood, unable to watch the terrible fate that was about to befall their daughter. "If I rescue your daughter," cried our hero, "will you give your blessing for us to be married?" The parents replied as one: "Yes, yes, a thousand times yes."

Remounting Pegasus, Perseus flew back into the air and flew towards the monster. With the sun behind him Perseus' shadow fell onto the sea. When the monster saw the shadow he tried to attack it. Seeing that the beast was otherwise engaged Perseus jumped from his horse and landed on the monster's back and struck a deep blow with his sword. It thrashed about wildly, roaring in anger and pain, but Perseus held firm. He struck again and again and soon the beast was dead. On the shore the king and queen shouted for joy. Perseus released Andromeda and carried her ashore, where she threw her arms around our hero while her parents greeted their new son-in-law.

The Prophecy

With Medusa's head secured in his bag, Perseus returned to Seriphos to introduce Andromeda to his mother. His mother was overjoyed to see them and hugged them tightly, but she then broke down in tears. "My son, I have terrible news," she said. "Polydectes is forcing me to marry him tomorrow."

Furious, Perseus left immediately for the palace. He burst into the great hall where the king and his friends were feasting and shouted: "Polydectes! Here is the gift you so dearly wanted!" And taking care to avert his eyes he pulled the gorgon's head from his bag and held it aloft. Everyone in the room bar Perseus looked up at the terrible trophy and all were immediately turned to stone, frozen in place for all time.

Rid of Polydectes, Perseus offered the head of Medusa in homage to Athena who attached it to her polished shield. He then returned the winged sandals, the helmet of invisibility and the bag that the nymphs had presented to him. Afterwards, with his mother and Andromeda, Perseus sought out his grandfather, old King Acrisius, to make up with him.

But when Acrisius heard that Perseus was on his way, he was terrified. He remembered the prophecy of the oracle so, to get away, he fled to the next town where some races and sporting competitions were being held.

Passing through the very same city was Perseus. Being an athletic young man, he was invited to take part in the discus event. When it came to his turn Perseus let fly with the discus with all his might. However, he was trying too hard and his discus veered off into the crowd where it struck the old king.

The blow killed the old man stone dead. Perseus had fulfilled the prophecy and completed his destiny – even if it was by accident. Perseus was now heir to the throne, but he had no wish to succeed the man he had killed. Instead he swapped his kingdom for one his cousin ruled and led a happy life with his wife and their many children.

When Perseus died, Zeus looked favourably upon him. Perseus had always shown the gods their due respect so Zeus made a constellation of stars appear in the sky, and from that day on they were called Perseus in his memory.

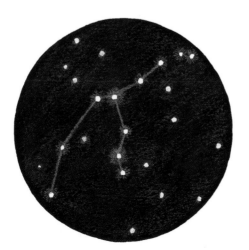

THE ADVENTURES OF ODYSSEUS

V ictory! After ten long years laying siege to the city of Troy, the Greeks had finally got inside. It was Odysseus' plan that got them in there – fifty warriors hidden inside the body of a large wooden horse which the Greeks left for the Trojans to find.

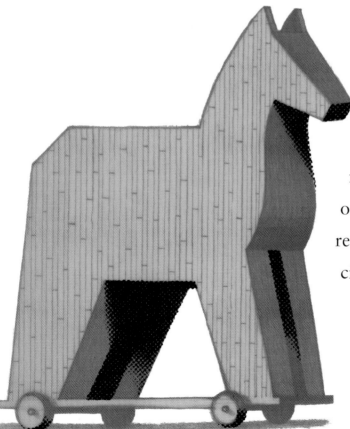

When the Trojans discovered the horse, abandoned on the sand, they took it back to their city thinking it was a gift from the gods. That night, the Greek warriors came out of the horse and, letting the rest of the Greek army into the city, conquered Troy.

There is Odysseus, triumphant at the head of the Greek fleet. His boats, loaded with treasure from Troy, sailed for his kingdom of Ithaca. He was also returning to his wife, Penelope and their child, Telemachus, who had not been born when Odysseus had left for Troy.

The boats made good speed across the seas and they had very nearly reached Ithaca when the weather turned against them. The gods were against the Greeks, so the waves crashed against their boats and the winds shredded their sails. The sailors tried to row ashore, but the lightning and thunder threw them back. The storm raged for nine days, but then on the tenth the seas were calm. Through the mist the sailors could see land.

The Awful Cyclops

As soon as the sailors came ashore they caught some wild goats which they cooked and ate. That night, while his exhausted sailors slept, Odysseus looked up at the hills and there he saw the silhouette of a person as big as a mountain. Now Odysseus was a curious man, so when dawn broke he ordered most of his men to stay with the boats while he took twelve of the bravest with him. "I must find out whether the people of this island are men like us," he said, "or savages that despise our gods."

Carrying a goatskin of strong wine the small band of warriors climbed up through the mountains until they reached a large cave. Odysseus entered first. "Look at all this," he cried. "Cheeses, milk, lamb; it must belong to a shepherd." The soldiers entered eager to try the food that Odysseus had found. But before anyone could lift a single morsel to their lips heavy footsteps shook the ground. And there at the mouth of the cave stood a giant as high as a mountain. It was a Cyclops, a one-eyed monster, called Polyphemus. The soldiers immediately ran to the back of the cave before Polyphemus could spot them. The Cyclops herded his sheep into the cave and rolled a rock over the entrance, not realising that he was imprisoning soldiers as well as sheep. "We're trapped!" thought a terrified Odysseus.

The Cyclops began to milk his sheep and it was then that he spotted the soldiers huddled at the back of his cave. "Who are you?" he roared. His voice alone struck fear into the warriors. "We are some of the Greek army returning from Troy," Odysseus replied. "The gods led us astray. I beg of you do not hurt us. In the name of Zeus we seek nothing more than some hospitality." Polyphemus laughed a long, cruel laugh. "You poor little man," he sneered, "don't you realise the Cyclops pay no heed to the gods. Zeus couldn't stop me from killing you if I wanted too." And with that he grabbed two of the Greek soldiers and devoured them there and then, one after the other. He then washed them down with a large jar of milk and fell asleep, content.

Odysseus grabbed his sword and was about to strike the Cyclops dead when a thought stopped him. "If I kill it now, we'll be trapped. A team of twenty horses couldn't shift the rock from the front of this cave."

When Polyphemus woke the next morning he ate two more Greek soldiers for breakfast before herding the sheep out of the cave. Unfortunately he rolled the rock back across the entrance before Odysseus and his comrades could escape. However, Odysseus struck upon a plan. Finding a long piece of wood he sharpened it to a point and then hid it in the shadows.

The evening came and Polyphemus returned. Again he devoured a pair of Greeks, but before he could drink some milk Odysseus spoke up. "Wait, Cyclops!" he said. "Try some of this." Odysseus held up some of the strong wine the Greeks had brought with them. "Why drink milk when you can have wine?" The giant took a drink. "I like this wine, little man," he said. "Tell me your name."

"I am called No-one," replied Odysseus, pouring the Cyclops another glass of wine. "A strange name," said Polyphemus, finishing that glass and beckoning for another. "I shall give you a gift in return." He drank another glass of wine and was by now really quite drunk. "My gift is . . . I shall . . . eat you last!" And with that the Cyclops collapsed into a drunken sleep.

As soon as the Cyclops was asleep, Odysseus grabbed the sharpened piece of wood he had hidden and drove the pointed end right into the centre of Polyphemus' one eye. The Cyclops jumped up and howled in pain. The noise was so loud it brought all the other Cyclops that lived round about dashing to the cave. "What is wrong?" they shouted. "Who has hurt you?" they asked. "No-one!" replied Polyphemus. "No-one has hurt me." When the other Cyclops heard this they walked off complaining: "If no one did anything why did you wake us up with your shouting?"

Polyphemus was enraged! He felt his way to the mouth of the cave and pushed the rock aside. Then the Cyclops stood there with his arms outstretched waiting for the Greeks as they tried to escape. Odysseus had a plan though. He tied the sheep together in threes and told his men to hold on to the underneath of the middle sheep. Odysseus herded the sheep out of the cave and then clung to the belly of the biggest ram in the flock. Polyphemus felt the sheep coming towards him and touched their backs as they passed to make sure the Greeks were not amongst them. Little did he suspect they were under them!

They were out and safe! The Greeks rushed down
the mountain and onto their boat. Odysseus could not
resist taunting the Cyclops. "Blind man!" he shouted.
"If you want to know who did this, it was me,
Odysseus, King of Ithaca and victor of Troy." Furious,
the Cyclops picked up a rock as big as a ship and
hurled it in Odysseus' direction. Fortunately the
boulder missed. Hearing the splash and knowing he
had failed, Polyphemus shouted to Poseidon, the god
of the seas: "Father, help me to get my revenge on
Odysseus!" Poseidon, who was indeed Polyphemus'
father, heard his son's call and vowed to do everything
in his power to stop Odysseus
returning home to Ithaca.

Circe the Magician

Odysseus' fleet arrived next at the Island of the Laestrygonians; a land of giant cannibals. They massacred the Greeks and only Odysseus' boat and crew survived. The survivors made it to another island and Odysseus sent a small search party to check it out.

The Greek scouts walked for a long time before coming upon a palace at the end of a valley. All around it were wild animals, and the soldiers drew their swords, prepared for an attack. Yet instead of jumping on the men, the lions and wolves rubbed against them, wanting to be stroked. Then a beautiful woman appeared at the door of the palace, and when she spoke her voice was as beguiling as her face. "I am Circe. Please come in, you must be thirsty." The men followed her and she poured them wine mixed with honey. What the Greeks did not realise was the wine was also mixed with a potion that would make them forget. As the men drank, Circe waved a wand and the men were turned into pigs.

When the search party didn't return, Odysseus began to get suspicious. Rather than risk any more of his crew he set off by himself to find his missing men. As he approached the palace his way was blocked by the god Hermes. "Take care Odysseus; that is the home of Circe the Magician. She turns any man that enters into a beast. She will do the same to you unless you eat this plant – it will protect you from her sorcery."

Odysseus thanked the god and ate the plant Hermes had given him. He then entered the palace and was met by Circe herself. As before she served wine mixed with honey and her magic potion. But this time when she waved her wand, nothing happened. Instead Odysseus drew his sword and grabbed Circe as if to kill her. "Ah, so you must be Odysseus," she said. "Hermes warned me that one day you would come and that you would be impervious to my spells."

"I can only love a man such as you," she continued. "Why not stay with me here in my palace." But Odysseus replied, "Circe, how can you talk of love when you have turned my crew into pigs? You must swear by the gods that you will release them from that terrible spell." Circe agreed and led Odysseus outside. There in a pigsty were his crew, rooting around in the straw looking for food. Circe smeared each pig in a special ointment and the pigs turned back into men – if anything the men looked slightly younger and better-looking than they were before they had met Circe.

The Greeks stayed in Circe's palace for a year and were well looked after. But Odysseus knew that he must return home. They bade farewell to Circe who warned them of the perils that might lie ahead.

The Land of the Dead

Circe had told Odysseus to seek the advice of the wise man Tiresias. Now Tiresias was dead, but by making sacrifices the Greeks could speak to those that dwelt in Hades, the land of the dead. As Odysseus sacrificed a ram he was surrounded by shadows; these were the dead and they came to taste the blood so that they might live for a while.

Amongst them were Tiresias and Odysseus' mother. Tiresias spoke: "So Odysseus, you want to know the truth?" he said.

"Poseidon means to do you harm for blinding his son, Polyphemus. He will go to great lengths to do so and will persecute you for as long as he is able. But if you overcome these tests you shall return to Ithaca."

Then the shadow that was Odysseus' mother spoke to him. "My son," she said in a soft voice, "you must know that Penelope believes you to be alive, but there is danger. Others say you are dead and are forcing her to remarry."

Tiresias spoke again. "If you want your men to be safe, forbid them to touch the sacred cows of Helios. I cannot say any more, for I am being called back to Hades." And with that the shadows disappeared back to the land of the dead.

The Sirens' Song

"Beware the Sirens," Circe had said. These frightening creatures were half woman, half bird and they entranced sailors with their beautiful song, only for the poor wretches to crash their boats on the rocks and die. As Odysseus' boat sailed near to where the Sirens lived he made his sailors stuff wax into their ears so that they would not hear the Sirens' song. Odysseus, on the other hand, did not block his ears. He was too curious to know what the Sirens' song sounded like. Instead he had his shipmates tie him to the mast. "Do not release me until we have passed the Sirens," he warned the crew. "And do not release me, even if I order it – in fact tie me tighter!"

Gradually, Odysseus began to hear a delicate sound on the winds.

It was the Sirens singing to him. Odysseus had never heard such a beautiful or melodious sound. "Come, come Odysseus," they sang, "Odysseus the Victorious, come and let us sing your praises and divulge to you our secrets." Odysseus was swamped with emotions that have no name. "Let me go!" he screamed. "Unfasten me at once!" The sailors could not hear him of course, but they could guess what he was saying, so they tightened his bonds instead.

When the ship was out of danger and Odysseus was untied, he fell to the deck sobbing with gratitude. "Thank you my friends," he said, "You have saved my life."

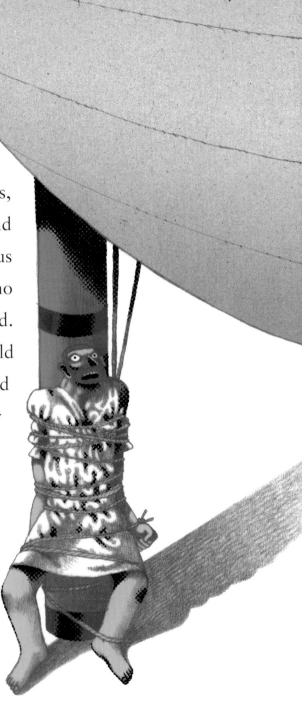

Charybdis and Scylla

The ship then had to sail between a swirling whirlpool and some rocks. The sailors strained at their oars as they tried to keep away from the pull of the whirlpool that would have dragged them to the monster Charybdis who lived there. In their efforts they came too close to the rocks and the six-headed monster that lived there called Scylla. It took one sailor in each mouth as they passed. Circe had warned Odysseus of these monsters. "You will avoid one only to become the prey of the other," she had said.

The Cattle of Helios

Exhausted, the crew landed on the island of the sun god, Helios. "Eat our provisions or fish," Odysseus instructed his men, "but under no circumstances touch the cattle you will find here, they belong to Helios." But one day, Odysseus was awoken from a sleep by the smell of cooking meat – his crew had disobeyed him!

"What are you doing?" screamed Odysseus. "Oh the things the gods will do to us now!" At that moment the bodies of the dead cows got up and walked around as if they were alive. The Greeks ran for their ship, but no sooner had they put to sea than the skies blackened and a terrible storm blew. The boat, battered by mountainous waves, sank. Everyone was lost to the raging seas but Odysseus, who had managed to grab on to a piece of wreckage. For nine days Odysseus clung on to that spar of wood, blistered by the sun, chilled by the night and stung by the salt of the sea, and then he fell into unconsciousness.

The Love of Calypso

When Odysseus opened his eyes there was a goddess looking at him. It was the nymph Calypso. She took Odysseus and cared for him, and in doing so fell in love with him. For seven years she kept him; and Odysseus could have been very happy, but all the while he could not forget his wife, Penelope. He would often go and sit on a rock by the edge of the sea and weep. One day Calypso found him on his rock. "Do not weep Odysseus," she said, "the gods have told me I have to let you go. But how can you love a mortal woman more than me, a goddess? I could have given you immortality. Eternal youth!" Odysseus looked at her. "Calypso you are a beautiful woman, but Penelope is the mother of my child and the woman that I love. The only thing I desire is to go home."

"In that case," replied Calypso, "I shall help you."

The Return to Ithaca

After many more tests, Odysseus arrived on a fog-bound beach. "Where am I?" he wondered. A woman appeared before him. It was Athena, the goddess of wisdom. "Odysseus," she said, "this is Ithaca; you are home. But be warned, things are not the same. You have been gone twenty years and most people believe you to be dead. The noblemen have only one thought – to marry Penelope and take your place. Until your wife decides upon which of these pretenders to marry, they all stay at your palace, feasting and squandering your wealth." Odysseus felt the anger welling up inside of him. "Penelope always believed you were alive," Athena continued. "She has tried many tricks to avoid getting married and has been successful all of this time. Her final idea was to say she could not marry until she had finished a magnificent tapestry. She works on it every day, but every night unpicks her stitches."

"However a maid has betrayed her and now the suitors demand she marries one of them this very week."

"I shall save her!" shouted Odysseus.

"Not so fast," replied Athena. "If the suitors see you they will kill you. Here's my plan; go to the hut of Eumaeus the swineherd disguised as a beggar. I will send your son, Telemachus, to meet you."

Telemachus Finds His Father

A little later Odysseus sat in Eumaeus' hut in disguise, when a good-looking young man arrived. "Is that you Prince Telemachus?" asked Eumaeus. "It is," replied the prince. "I will tell you about my journey, but first tell my mother not to worry and that I am safe." Eumaeus left to do the prince's bidding.

At that moment Athena cast a spell which transformed Odysseus from his disguise to his true self. Telemachus was astounded. "Are you a god that you can change your appearance so?" he asked. Odysseus laughed. "No my boy, it is I, Odysseus, your father. It was Athena who disguised me." I am here to seek your help against the pretenders to my throne, but I beg of you, do not tell anyone I am here."

Father and son hugged each other and wept tears of joy. They plotted their revenge, and then Telemachus returned to the palace as if nothing had happened.

The Arrival at the Palace

A while later Odysseus, disguised again as a beggar, made his way to the palace escorted by Eumaeus. No sooner had he entered than a dog came running towards him barking happily. The dog was so old that the effort killed it. Odysseus wept quietly, for it was his dog, Argos, and it had still recognised him after twenty years. Odysseus entered a great hall, where the suitors were feasting. Telemachus invited him to sit at the table and eat. But the suitors gave Odysseus scraps, some offered only insults – and one threw a stool at the beggar's head!

Penelope was horrified to see a poor beggar being so abused under her own roof. She beckoned him over, and he saw again how beautiful she was. Odysseus remained in the shadows though, so he would not be discovered. When she asked him who he was, he disguised his voice and made up a tale of how he had been travelling and that he had met Odysseus and that he would return soon to Ithaca. On hearing this the tears streamed down Penelope's cheeks. "I hope you speak the truth," she said, "for I would like that very much; it has been so long."

Penelope instructed a old maid to take Odysseus to the baths so he might have a wash. When he was getting undressed the maid spotted a scar on his leg. "Odysseus!" she cried. "It is you! You cannot fool your old nurse – you got that scar from a wild boar when you were but a child." She wept with happiness but Odysseus made her swear to keep his presence in Ithaca a secret.

The Massacre of the Pretenders

The next day Penelope, in an idea inspired by Athena, held a competition. She stood at one end of the great hall and held up a bow. "This is Odysseus' bow," she said. "I will marry whoever can string it and then fire a single arrow through a line of twelve axe-heads."

The suitors all lined up to try, but not one of them came close to completing the task. Then Odysseus asked for permission to try. The pretenders all laughed when they saw this.

"Look at the old fool," they said. "He can barely stand by himself, yet he thinks he can win himself a queen."

"How dare you offend my guest," snapped Penelope. "You are ashamed you failed and fear that this man may do what you could not." And she strode from the hall.

Odysseus picked up the stiff old bow and strung it with ease. Then, taking an arrow, he fired it clean through the line of axe heads. The suitors were dumbfounded, but their surprise turned to terror as Odysseus whipped off his disguise. "Yes, it is I, Odysseus!" he cried, "And you who have abused my wealth and tormented my wife shall pay for your treachery with your lives!" And the wrath of Odysseus fell upon the suitors and, aided by Telemachus and the will of the gods, he slaughtered them all.

The Couple's Secret

After clearing the hall, Odysseus sent his old nurse to find Penelope and tell her the news. "Come, come, Odysseus has returned," she called when she found Penelope, but the queen did not believe her. "Trust me," said the nurse, "I have seen his scar – he was disguised as the beggar and he has killed all the suitors."

Her heart racing, Penelope went to the great hall and looked upon Odysseus. She studied the face of the man standing in front of her for a long time, but did not say a word. It was too much for Telemachus.

"Mother is your heart frozen?" he cried. "Why don't you say anything?"

Penelope turned to her son. "I fear that this is just a trick," she said. "But I know a way of testing this man. Odysseus and I know

a secret that will prove if this man is genuine or not. In the meantime I shall ask for a servant to move my bed from my room so our guest can take a rest." "Take out the bed?" asked Odysseus. "That's impossible! One foot of the bed is part of an olive tree that grows in the palace. I built the room with my own hands and left the tree there. Only you and I know that."

That was the secret that Penelope had talked of. Crying with joy she threw her arms around her husband. "Are you cross with me for testing you?" asked Penelope. Instead Odysseus praised her for her clever test.

They held each other all night not wishing to be separated again; and the gods smiled upon them and granted them long, happy lives together.